Food Stylist

ODD
JOBS

VIRGINIA LOH-HAGAN

45th Parallel Press

Published in the United States of America by Cherry Lake Publishing
Ann Arbor, Michigan
www.cherrylakepublishing.com

Content Adviser: Kristen Miglore, Creative Director, Food52, New York, NY
Reading Adviser: Marla Conn MS, Ed., Literacy specialist, Read-Ability, Inc.

Photo Credits: © Fotografiche/Shutterstock, cover, 1; © Laoshi/istock, 5; © Stock-Asso/Shutterstock, 6; © Dario Diament/Shutterstock, 9; © Photowitch | Dreamstime.com - Cookbook Reading Photo, 11; © Kiryl Padabed/Shutterstock, 12; © logoff/istock, 14; © holbox/Shutterstock, 17; © Syda Productions/Shutterstock, 19; © Roman Seliutin/Shutterstock, 20; © TNPhotographer/Shutterstock, 23; © mediaphotos/istock, 25; © fuzznails/istock, 27; © Flashon Studio/Shutterstock, 28; © ARENA Creative/Shutterstock, cover, multiple interior pages; © oculo/Shutterstock, multiple interior pages; © Denniro/Shutterstock.com, cover, multiple interior pages; © PhotoHouse/Shutterstock, multiple interior pages; © Miloje/Shutterstock, multiple interior pages

45th Parallel Press is an imprint of Cherry Lake Publishing.

Library of Congress Cataloging-in-Publication Data

Names: Loh-Hagan, Virginia, author. | Loh-Hagan, Virginia. Odd jobs.
Title: Food stylist / by Virginia Loh-Hagan.
Description: Ann Arbor, MI : Cherry Lake Publishing, [2016] | Series: Odd
   jobs | Includes bibliographical references and index.
Identifiers: LCCN 2015050674| ISBN 9781634710954 (hardcover) |
   ISBN 9781634712934 (pbk.) | ISBN 9781634711944 (pdf) |
   ISBN 9781634713924 (ebook)
Subjects: LCSH: Food presentation—Juvenile literature. | Photography of
   food—Juvenile literature. | Food industry and trade—Vocational
   guidance—Juvenile literature.
Classification: LCC TX740.5 .L64 2016 | DDC 641.30023—dc23
LC record available at http://lccn.loc.gov/2015050674

Cherry Lake Publishing would like to acknowledge the work of The Partnership for 21st Century Skills.
Please visit *www.p21*.org for more information.

Printed in the United States of America
Corporate Graphics Inc.

Contents

CHAPTER 1

The Art of Food Styling

Who are famous food stylists? How are they artists, problem solvers, and magicians?

Mary Valentin plays with food. And she gets paid for it! She's a food stylist. She uses real food. She makes it look awesome.

She studied art. She was painting backgrounds. A food stylist asked for help. She didn't know about food styling. She said, "But they offered to pay me. So I showed up." She was hooked.

She said, "The food stylist has a deep understanding of food." She makes food look yummy. She wants people to imagine how food smells and tastes.

Food propping is making food to support the main dish being photographed.

Big companies hire her. They **shoot** her food. Shoot means takes a picture. She gets people to buy food. She makes food into art.

Adam Pearson is a food stylist. He creates beautiful food photos. He creates them for catalogs and magazines. He creates them for cookbooks. He works hard. Each project takes time.

Food stylists write menu notes. These notes improve the recipes.

MARIANA VELASQUEZ

Mariana Velasquez is a food stylist. Her work has been featured in many magazines, cookbooks, and ads. She's from Colombia. She went to Big Sur, California. She pursued her dream of tasting, cooking, and writing about food. She went to cooking school. She went to New York City. She started as a taster. She liked the "visual side" of food. Then, she became a food stylist. She worked with a mentor. She's inspired by art and fashion. She draws the food first. She imagines what the food looks like. She said, "I love projects where I read the recipes and my mouth waters." She travels the world. She finds recipes.

He gathers **recipes**. Recipes explain how to make food dishes. They include steps. They include **ingredients**. Ingredients are things needed to make a dish.

He makes shopping lists. He meets with his team. He cooks. He styles food. He puts food on plates. He takes food to the **set**. A set is at the studio. He said, "That's where the real magic happens."

He said, "Food styling is five percent **technique**, five percent magic, and five percent problem solving." Technique is skill.

Lisa Heathcote is a chef. She's also a food stylist. She works for movies. She works for television. She worked on *Downton Abbey*.

All the food is real. She said, "If you have fake food, it's going to look like fake food."

She stays true to history. She creates food that would've been eaten at the time. Fish was popular. But seafood isn't good for filming. It smells. So, Heathcote solved that problem. She used chicken. She made chicken look like fish. She cut it in different ways. She made different sauces. She practiced. She made many versions.

Food stylists make magic. They trick people's eyes. They create with food.

It can take many people to help get the perfect shot.

CHAPTER 2

Playing with Food

What do food stylists do? What tools do they use? What techniques do they use?

Food stylists prepare food. They get food ready to be **shot**. A shot is a photograph. They take **still lifes**. A still life is a picture of an object. Their photos are used to sell food. They're used in movies and television.

Food stylists make food look delicious. They glue food together. They pin food. They arrange food. They present food.

Kim Kissling wins awards. She loves food. She uses fresh food. She said, "My job is simply to make food look beautiful … it usually takes a lot of people to make it a success."

Food photos are used in ads, magazines, menus, cookbooks, movies, and television.

Food stylists work with a team. They work with photographers. They work with assistants. They work with directors. They work together. They prep. They shoot. They clean.

Food stylists use many tools. They use sharp knives. They make exact cuts.

They use small scissors. They cut. They trim edges. They get into small spaces. They use **stencils**.

Food stylists need tiny tools to help them work with small food items.

Stencils are cut-outs that help make patterns. They're used for decorating.

Stylists use rulers. They measure. They want things to be even.

They use brushes. They dust surfaces. They brush away dust. They brush away powder.

They use **spatulas**. Spatulas are flat scrapers. They smooth things. They spread icing.

Stylists use **tweezers**. They grab things. They move around small objects. They lower items. They pull out items.

They use glue. They sew. They put things together. They make things stick.

Food stylists have special skills. Their skills are like tricks.

Some foods are **stacked**. Stacked means piled up. Food stylists work with pancakes. They work with burgers. They use cardboard. They use toothpicks. These support layers.

They spray food. This makes food look fresh. They work with turkeys. Sometimes they use raw turkeys.

But they look cooked. Food stylists spray color. They spray oil. They stuff using paper towels. Turkeys look plump. They shine.

Sometimes they use things to look like food. They use glue for milk. They use plastic cubes for ice. They use soap for soda bubbles.

Food stylists use many ingredients. They test ingredients for shoots.

Food Stylist
KNOW THE LINGO

Alive: food that looks fresh and ready to shoot

Dead: food that needs to be replaced or refreshed

Dollop: a nicely placed blob or lump

Drip: a shot that shows a drip falling

How-tos: shots that show how to do something; a series of shots

Pour: a shot that shows something being poured onto something else

Pre-pro: meeting before a photo shoot

Pulled back: showing atmosphere and the food

Skirt: ice cream at the base of a scoop of ice cream in a cone

Spritz: spraying water onto food to make it look fresh and cold

Stand-in food: food that serves as a placement until the set is perfect

Tabletop: shot that includes a table setting and food

Talent: people featured in a shot

Tight on the food: making sure food is the main focus of a shot

Wrap time: the time of day that the shoot finishes

CHAPTER 3

Becoming a Food Stylist

How does one learn to be a food stylist? What do food stylists need to learn?

Delores Custer loves working with food. This started at a young age. She watched cooking shows. She took cooking classes. She opened a restaurant. She got a master's degree. She studied food science. She studied art. She studied design.

She worked for a food stylist. She learned about the job. She said, "I assisted and learned from one of the best." She learned many skills. Then, she started her own business.

She said, "We are hired because of our skills, our personalities, and how we arrange food." She's creative. She has fun with food.

Food stylists should put together an album of their work.

Food stylists learn about food. They learn about art. They're trained **image** specialists. Image is how people see something. Food stylists create how people see food.

There are several good cooking schools. They offer food styling programs. They teach **plating**. Plating is

Advice From the Field
LOUISE LEONARD

Louise Leonard is a food stylist. She won a television cooking show. She works for television shows. She teaches food styling. She loves to travel. She loves to explore. She cooks using things she learned around the world. She loves styling and shooting food. The most important part of her job is shopping. She told her students, "I hope you liked going on scavenger hunts as a kid. I spend the majority of my time running around to every supermarket, farmer's market, specialty store, butcher shop, bakery, florist, [and] prop house, schlepping groceries all over the place, calling to source weird ingredients that aren't in season, and so forth."

presenting the food. Lisa Schoen is a teacher. She's an expert on plating camera-ready food.

Food stylists teach their own classes. Jacqueline Buckner teaches private lessons. She works with small groups. She works with individuals.

There are online classes. Some people can't meet in person. They train online. They practice at home.

Food stylists learn the newest skills. They learn the newest trends.

Food stylists can get certificates.

Food stylists don't like to waste food if they don't have to.

Many food stylists learn from **mentors**. Mentors are more experienced. New stylists assist other food stylists. They practice. They get experience. They gain contacts.

They learn how to shop. They look for the best items. They look for the best prices.

They learn how to do a shoot. They set up. They take test shots. They prepare backgrounds.

They learn about lighting. Jennifer Joyce said, "Good lighting is essential for a good food photo." Yellow lights aren't good. They make food look ugly. Natural light is the best. Stylists like taking shots by windows.

CHAPTER 4

Plates to Pics

Who is Donna Hay? How did food photography change and develop?

Donna Hay changed food photography. She's from Australia. She's in charge of a magazine. She's a food stylist. She introduced **selective** focus. Selective means to be specific. Hay made food the center of attention. She did this in the 1990s.

She did close-ups of food. She shot from above. She shot from the side. Her shots were simple. They were clean. They were bright. They were colorful.

Photo styles changed. But food photos stayed popular. There were more food magazines.

Supermarkets started their own magazines. More cookbooks had photos. There were more cooking shows. There's more demand for food photos.

Taking pictures of food became more popular in the 1990s.

WHEN ODD IS TOO ODD!

Stephen McMennamy is a food photographer. He takes "combophotos." He uses his imagination. He combines images. He combines two unrelated objects. He combines food with things. His first image was a banana and the Empire State Building. He said, "It instantly got me wondering what else was out there to tinker with." He combined Froot Loops and an old dump truck. He combined an orange and a naked man. He combined a forklift with a giant hot dog. He combined a fire extinguisher with a shiny red jalapeño pepper. He combined cigarettes and French fries. He said, "I felt like a food stylist."

In 2004, new ads came out. A company made food more fun. Its ads focused on movement. They focused on **texture**. Texture is how something feels. It's how something is shaped.

Cheese oozed out. Eggs spun. Shrimp curled on the grill. Olive oil dripped down bread. Berries exploded.

Food is the star. It's the **hero**. Hero food is the main food. It's featured in a shot.

Food stylists help. They make food more eye-catching.

Today, everyone is a photographer. People use phones to take pictures. They take lots of food pictures. They post them online.

Good food photos take a long time to style.

CHAPTER 5

Fighting Food Fakery

What don't some people like food styling? How are food stylists addressing food fakery?

Some people don't like food styling. They think it's a lie. Food stylists make food look better than it is. People don't like that.

Passing off fake food as real is **illegal**. This means it's against the law. A company got in trouble. It was blamed for not selling what they photographed.

So, things changed. There's a rule. The hero food has to be real. The food around the hero can be fake.

Food stylists are careful about **portions**. Portion is serving size. They're careful about content. They stay true to the food.

Today's food styling has little **fakery**. Fakery is the process of faking things.

People like food that looks like it came from a farm, not a lab.

People want more natural foods. Healthy eating is popular. Food stylists use more natural food. This means the food is not perfect. Natural food is smaller. It's duller. It has odd shapes. It may be bruised.

Messy food is popular. Food stylists make food look messy. They don't want the perfect look. They allow pie filling to ooze out. They shoot pies with slices removed. They leave crumbs. They leave drips.

Food styling is an odd job. It's also a yummy job!

Today, styled food looks alive.

THAT HAPPENED?!?

Janice Poon is a food stylist. She worked on a television show. It was about a man who eats humans! So, she made dishes that looked like human parts. She asked, "Where am I going to get an animal that passes as a human being that's going to be credible?" She tried to get giraffe meat. She called a few zoos! That didn't work. So, she got creative. She sewed different meats together. She put one kind of meat on a different bone. She had to make a human leg dish. She sewed pork muscle over the leg bones of a baby cow and lamb. She wrapped it with leaves. She decorated it with fruits and flowers. She said, "I want ... the food to look so delicious that you want to reach into the screen and try it."

DID YOU KNOW?

- Dishes with patterns are distracting. Colorful dishes are distracting. They take away from the food. Plain plates show off food the best.

- Melissa McSorley styles food for movies. She worked on *Chef*. She made Cubanos. Cubanos are special sandwiches. She and her team made about 800 Cubanos.

- A food stylist went to Florida. The food stylist took pictures of orange trees. The trees didn't have enough fruit. The food stylist sewed oranges to the branches.

- Shooting pizza is hard. The "cheese pull" is a hard trick. Food stylists use boiling water. They use steam. They melt the cheese. Then, they pull the cheese.

- Food stylists need to freeze ice cream. If there is no freezer they use buckets of dry ice.

- Mari Williams worked for a company that sells rice. She had to handpick the rice for a photo shoot. She needed rice of a certain size, shape, and color. She arranged them with tweezers. It was a slow process.

- Emily Marshall is a food stylist. She collects old cookbooks. She works on a television show. The show is about astronauts. She made a meat loaf that looks like the moon. It's called a Lunar Loaf.

CONSIDER THIS!

TAKE A POSITION! Technology has changed food photographing and styling. Everyone can take pictures. They can easily make corrections. Are food stylists still necessary? Argue your point with reasons and evidence.

SAY WHAT? Food stylists have tricks of the trade. They make food look good. Explain some ways food stylists make food look fresh. Explain why they did this.

THINK ABOUT IT! Some people think food styling is wasteful. It takes many shots to get a good picture. Lots of food is wasted. Many people are starving. Should food stylists be allowed to waste food? What do you think about this?

SEE A DIFFERENT SIDE! Reread Chapter 5. It's entitled "Fighting Food Fakery." This is another perspective on food styling. Do you agree or disagree with this point of view?

LEARN MORE: RESOURCES

PRIMARY SOURCE

Freymann, Saxton, and Joost Elfers. *Food Play*. San Francisco: Chronicle Books, 2006.

Parks-Whitfield, Alison. *Food Styling & Photography for Dummies*. Hoboken, NJ: Wiley, 2012.

SECONDARY SOURCE

National Geographic Kids—Food That Fools You: http://kids.nationalgeographic.com/explore/food-that-fools-you/

WEB SITES

Food Stylist and Food Styling Directory: http://foodportfolio.com/food_stylists/

International Association of Culinary Professionals—Food Photographers & Stylists: https://www.iacp.com/connect/more/food_photographers_stylists

GLOSSARY

fakery (FAY-kuh-ree) the process of faking or lying

hero (HEER-oh) the main food, the food that is actually in the photograph, not the test or practice food

illegal (ih-LEE-guhl) against the law

image (IM-ij) how something appears

ingredients (in-GREE-dee-uhnts) the things needed to make a dish

mentors (MEN-turz) experts who train others

plating (PLAY-ting) putting food on a plate and presenting it

portions (POR-shunz) serving size

recipes (RES-uh-peez) ingredients and steps for making a food dish

selective (suh-LEK-tiv) specific, picky

set (SET) at the studio, where a photo shoot takes place

shoot (SHOOT) takes a photograph; a photo session

shot (SHAHT) photographed; a picture, a photo

spatulas (SPACH-uh-luhz) flat tools used for smoothing or scraping

stacked (STAKD) piled up

stencils (STEN-suhlz) cut-outs to help make patterns for decorating

still lifes (STIL LIFEZ) photos of objects that aren't moving

technique (tek-NEEK) skill

texture (TEKS-chur) how something feels or is shaped

tweezers (TWEE-zurz) a tool used to grab things

INDEX

ABOUT THE AUTHOR

Dr. Virginia Loh-Hagan is an author, university professor, former classroom teacher, and curriculum designer. She loves eating food, styled or not. She lives in San Diego with her very tall husband and very naughty dogs. To learn more about her, visit www.virginialoh.com.

WITHDRAWN